LYRICS of LIFE

Volume II

By Billie Ambers

Lyrics of Life

By Billie Ambers

Volume II

Trademark

Lyrics of Life Publications

Los Angeles, California 90008

Lyrics of Life Publications
Los Angeles, California 90008

Telephone (323) 792-4446   Facsimile (323) 792-4446

Books Online: www.Amazon.com

E-Mail Address: LyricsOfLife@SBCglobal.net

Lyrics of Life revised and reprinted, 2023.
Copyrights © 1995 and 2008 by Billie Ambers.
Compiled from original poems composed by Billie Ambers.

All rights reserved under International Copyright Law.
Written permission must be secured from the Publisher to use or reproduce
this book in any form; contents and/or cover, whole or in part.

Published in Los Angeles, California, by Lyrics of Life Publications.
Distributed by Lyrics of Life Publications, Los Angeles, California.

Library of Congress Cataloging in Publication Data

Ambers, Billie
    Lyrics of Life by Billie Ambers.

    Original Poems by Billie Ambers.
    Lyrics of Life Publications.
    ISBN 0-9653400-0-7
    UPC 61220500001-5
    Trademark Reg. No. 3761030 Serial No. 77795226

Biblical references from teachings of Holy Bibles.

Majority of Pictures by Ed Simpson Stock Photography.

Printed in the United States of America.

ACKNOWLEDGEMENTS

A special gratefulness and thankfulness to:

God for His divine guidance and grace, the Lord Christ Jesus for His gifts, and the Holy Spirit for His anointing; whereby I was given the inspiration and ability to write these poetic lyrics.

DEDICATION

To the memory of my two beloved sons

Dwayne Mandel
and
Derrick Craig

Whose courage inspires me continuously,
Whose love lives with me daily,
Whose joyousness warms my heart,
Whose names are written in the Book of Life,
Who have resided in the Father's mansion,
Since, December, eighth, nineteen-ninety,
And, November, seventh, 2003, respectively.

CONTENTS

Title	Page
Preface	xiii
Life	2
Serenity	4
Battling The Bulge	6
Freedom Is Never Free	8
California Vacation	10
Success	12
A Genius The World Beholds	14
Fun In the Sun	16
A Precious Grandchild	18
The Old Homestead	20
Bereavement Comfort	22
The Ocean	24
Looking For Mister Right	26
Amazing Autumn	28
The Enlistment	30
Grandpa's Birthday Bash	32
The Proposal	34
My Best Friend	36
Only A Season	38
Lovers Meet Again	40
Spa Enchantment	42

CONTENTS

Title	Page
It's My Fault, Not His.	44
The Backyard Barbeque	46
I've Got To Have Her	48
United We Stand	50
Winter's Bliss	52
The Wedding	54
Thanksgiving At Grandma's	56
Compulsions	58
Missed Opportunities	60
Spring Is Here	62
The Honeymoon	64
Being Your Best	66
Convicted Without A Charge	68
Retirement	70
The Introduction	72
Christmas Season	74
Mother, Mom, Love	76
Love	78
Karma The Mega Bummer	80
He Is A Dandy	82
Remembering	84
Still, The Child Cries	86

CONTENTS

Title	Page
Love At First Sight	88
New Year's Celebration	90
The Other Woman	92
Relaxation	94
The Wedding Anniversary	96
The Equalizer	98
Education Is A Tool	100
Genuine Agony	102
My First Date	104
Situations	106
Lost Love	108
She Is Needy	110
Easy On My Eyes	112
The Final Decree	114
Valentine's Day	116
Searching For My Significant Other	118
Alone, But Not Lonely	120
Serial Marriages	122
Crime In America	124
Only Thirteen	126
Loving Life	128
Life Everlasting	130

PREFACE

Lyrics of Life is a book that represents life experiences in a poetic style. The poems in this book begin with "Life" and conclude with "Life Everlasting," and a variety of topics on life are presented in poetic form between these two bookends.

Lyrics of Life is a work of art in poems, pictures, and presentation. The objective of these lyrical works is to encourage, motivate, and entertain you. The poems in this book are intended to enable you to derive enjoyment, inspiration, and enlightenment delightfully.

Lyrics of Life has full-page color photography of landscapes, ocean views, and floral scenery that complement each poem to provide splendor and visionary depth for the lyrics of these works. The goal of this book is to present a multiplicity of life related experiences in an insightful and pleasurable manner.

May you immensely enjoy the poems and photography in *Lyrics of Life*.

Billie Ambers

Life

Life is a growth process,
Comparable to a ladder.
When we have reached one step,
The next one is even higher.

Life is ever evolving,
With peaks and valleys.
When you have arrived at a peak,
Be sure to prepare for the valley.

Life is an obstacle course,
With blockades and barriers.
When we have conquered one,
It strengthens us for another.

Life is ever elusive,
Providing constant excitement.
When we think we have it analyzed,
It presents us with new surprises!

Life is especially enchanting,
Presenting perpetual questions.
When we attempt to provide answers,
It leads us to other inquisitions.

Life is most interesting,
And it provides a constant challenge.
If one lives to be one hundred,
One has barely touched the surface.

Life is our most precious possession,
And it is very fragile.
Life is our greatest blessing,
And it should be treasured!

Serenity

The day has a cast of magnificence,
And an engrossing charm.
It is mesmerizing and blissfully calm,
And lives with one affectionately in the heart.

The air is clean and crisp,
Touching one caressingly.
Tranquility permeates the atmosphere,
The scene is like a wonderful fantasy.

The sun is shining charismatically brilliant,
A soft breeze whispers gently on the face,
Giving one a gracious embrace.
The peace expresses comfort and ecstasy.

The mountains stand inspiringly sculptured,
The sky is a splendid blue.
The birds are gliding gracefully,
As they fly by chirping cheerfully.

The crystal clear stream is softly flowing,
As it sparkles and glistens.
It is cascading gracefully,
Its water trickling musically.

The colorful rock sediments,
Lay resting on its bed.
The ambiance is captivating,
The serenity is embracing.

The pristine stream is delicately rippling,
Over strikingly beautiful sediments.
Trout leap flickering in it,
And dive with a splash swimming rapidly.

The flowers are gorgeously beautiful,
Their brightness clearly glorious.
The plants are wonderfully colorful,
Expressing their splendor elegantly.

The tree leaves are playfully swaying,
Softly tinkling in the breeze.
The foliage displays a brilliant hue,
For the squirrels to scamper sporadically through.

Rabbits are romping through the chartreuse grass,
Squirrels pause to quickly rub acorns.
The serenity of this lovely site,
Lives indelibly in the heart.

Battling The Bulge

The desserts are appealing,
The waistline is crawling,
Oh, the inches it has attained,
The mind says, no,
But the will power is game!

The cocktails are calling,
The midriff is appalling,
Oh, the expansion it contains,
The mind says, no,
But the will power is aflame!

The calories are mounting,
The tummy's ceased growling,
Oh, the inches are disdained,
The mind says, no,
But the will power is not tame!

The cholesterol has warnings,
The appetite is drooling,
Oh, the desire should be restrained,
The mind says, no,
But the will power does not abstain!

The bread is beckoning,
The appetite is besetting,
Oh, just tidbits are proclaimed,
The mind says, no,
But the will power is drained!

The chocolates are shouting,
The desire is howling,
Oh, growth the body has pertained,
The mind says, no,
But the will power is insane!

Control these obsessions,
The mind has possession,
And recognizes compulsions refrained.
The mind has these impulses contained,
Now the will power is maintained!

Freedom Is Never Free

Our military forces are dedicated and stalwart,
Expertly skilled with willing minds and loyal hearts.
Exceptional men and women who protect our shores,
We are blessed to have our supreme military corps.

These brave heroes pay such a horrendous price,
As they sacrifice their bodies, limbs, and lives.
These valiant soldiers exhibit the greatest generosity,
We are deeply grateful for their steadfast loyalty.

Many soldiers' lives have been severely altered,
Families holding military funerals for the fallen.
American lives have been given for our liberty,
We are ever aware that freedom is never free!

Our soldiers brave commitment we shall always honor,
Their triumphant victories we will always savor.
Our superb military forces are exceedingly stellar,
We salute our veterans for their services and valor.

Our military forces exemplify magnanimous courage,
They persevere for us to ensure our blessed freedom.
While our forces are on battlefields of perils,
We must always support them with fervent prayers.

May our soldiers be safe, protected, and shielded,
On the land, in the air, and on the seas continuously.
Bring them home safely for they fight to keep us free,
We are ever proud of them and thankful perpetually.

Many soldiers' lives have been severely altered,
Families holding military funerals for the fallen.
American lives have been given for our liberty,
We are ever aware that freedom is never free!

California Vacation

Why don't we plan our vacation,
We need the rest and relaxation.
Let's drive to beautiful balmy San Diego,
Watch the Padres and visit a SeaWorld Show.

We will drive along the picturesque coastline route,
Visit Laguna Beach and stay at a seaside resort.
Have a tropical breakfast on a gorgeous ocean bluff,
Relax on the beach as the waves break onto the shore.

Cruise to Los Angeles and visit the Marina,
Sail to have a day on the Island of Catalina.
Return to Beverly Hills for a shopping spree,
Visit Hollywood to see the movie studios mystique.

Drive to lovely Carmel by the seashore,
Stay in a bed and breakfast with an ocean view.
Visit the museums and exquisite art exhibits,
Enjoy the unique boutiques in this quaint city.

Meander to San Francisco by the scenic ocean route,
Stroll along the boardwalk at Fisherman's Wharf.
Attend a concert and great ballet performance,
Dine at The Ritz-Carlton for a romantic dinner.

Proceed to Sacramento to tour the State Capitol,
Visit historical sites that are vividly insightful.
Go through Yosemite Park and see its redwood forest,
Stupendous trees standing majestically all around us.

We will have such an eventful vacation,
And reluctantly end our fabulous recreation.
We will say farewell for the time being,
Surely we will return next year to visit again.

Success

Success is having a commitment,
Toward ones aspirations.
It is meeting obligations,
And seizing opportunities.

Success is defining objectives,
And remaining focused.
It is challenging abilities,
On unknown excursions.

Success is demonstrating courage,
Under adverse conditions.
It is being dedicated,
And deferring gratifications.

Success requires perseverance,
And a firm declaration.
It demands tenacity,
Through difficult circumstances.

Success is developing self-discipline,
And acquiring self-motivation.
It is setting attainable goals,
And being goal-oriented.

Success is having the fortitude,
To embark upon new adventures.
It is striving for excellence,
And achieving new accomplishments.

Success is eliminating excuses,
And having a strong determination.
It is developing confidence,
And having a strong constitution.

A Genius The World Beholds
(Ray Charles)

He lived in darkness,
With sightless eyes,
Yet he was known a genius,
In his own lifetime.

Lowly and humbly he did arrive,
Strength and perseverance helped him survive.
His mother's love and wisdom as his guide,
The gifts of God abundantly magnified.

Silent tears for a tragic loss,
Dreadful pain, but not his fault.
Suffered blight and a stain untold,
He excelled to heights the world beholds.

His gifts of music quite a mystique,
His auditory sensory most unique.
Instruments and singing in his head,
Yet he hears the hovering of a hummingbird.

A genius doing what was impossible,
In music and business he was incomparable.
With vocals penetrating the heart and spine,
His soulful songs crossing all spectrums in life.

Silent tears for a tragic loss,
Dreadful pain, but not his fault.
Suffered blight and a stain untold,
He excelled to heights the world beholds.

Musical genius ever classic abound,
Accolades that are ever renowned.
His songs mostly platinum and gold,
He excelled to heights the world beholds!

Fun In The Sun

Cruising along in my vintage car,
Arriving at the beach that is not too far.
Lying on the warm white sand,
Enjoying the sun while getting a tan.

Listening to waves splashing onto the shore,
Wishing to do this quite a bit more.
Watching surfers ride their boards,
Causing lifeguards to perform their chores.

Soaking up the bright warm sun,
Seeing kids playing and having fun.
Strolling along the water's edge,
Clearing the tension from my head.

Stopping to watch the volleyball game,
Hoping someday to do the same.
Reaching the nearest hotdog stand,
Getting cotton candy all over my hands.

Joining groups in beach picnics,
Laughing and joking gives me a kick.
Eating delicious foods and tasty snacks,
Munching icy popsicles on a stick.

Having such fun is quite a treat,
Expecting future visits to be a repeat.
Feeling great and very relaxed,
Knowing I will soon be coming back.

Pausing to experience the lovely sunset,
Remembering all the people I have met.
Leaving with the homebound crowd,
Planning to return when the weekend comes around.

A Precious Grandchild

Bright face with eyes aglow,
Hands and feet wave joyfully,
A smile that makes the heart serene,
'Tis God's blessed gift to me,
A precious grandchild, you see.

Wobbly legs with first steps totter,
Moddly hand, a familiar scene,
A squeal, a giggle, and a blush supreme,
'Tis God's blessed gift to me,
A precious grandchild, you see.

The first day of school is at hand,
My, so many rules to understand,
Face lit with eagerness and glee,
'Tis God's blessed gift to me,
A precious grandchild, you see.

Adolescence, after pre-teens,
Oh, what a lifestyle is seen,
Where independence reigns supreme,
'Tis God's blessed gift to me,
A precious grandchild, you see.

College summons soon,
Well, look who we have groomed,
For a professional now blooms,
'Tis God's blessed gift to me,
A precious grandchild, you see.

Wedding bells to ring their chimes,
Vows to be exchanged on time,
Beautiful ever is this scene,
'Tis God's blessed gift to me,
A precious grandchild, you see.

When the twilight years appear,
When other things grow dim, though near,
My inspiration will always be,
God's blessed gift to me,
A precious grandchild, you see.

The Old Homestead

Remembrance and thoughts of yesterday,
Living life at a much slower pace.
A plank board shanty on a southern farm,
Roosters crowing at the break of dawn.

Mother's in the kitchen making bread,
Rising early to assure the family is fed.
Baking homemade biscuits and butter rolls,
Delicious meals cooking on the oil fueled stove.

Pork chops, corn grits, and sugar cured hams,
Mustard greens, string beans, and candied yams;
Fried chicken, gravy, and hot water cornbread,
Heartfelt remembrance of the old homestead.

Daddy's tending cows for the milk he sells,
Drawing water daily from the deep cool well.
Plowing hot fields in the red clay soil,
Planting seasonal crops through much toil.

Mother's washing clothes in the big tin tub,
Scrubbed clean laboriously on the old rub board.
Washpot brewing to make the clothes sanitized,
Clothes swaying in the wind hanging on wirelines.

Potbellied stove in the middle of the floor,
Keeping the house toasty when the fire is stoked.
Grandma's making quilts and patching pants,
Knitting sweaters and mittens with loving hands.

A giant walnut tree providing food and shade,
A wonderful cozy place for us kids to play.
Warm loving memories of a different day,
Heartfelt remembrance of the old homestead.

Bereavement Comfort

Though our loved one has fallen asleep,
God will give us a deep inner peace.
May you stand firmly on His Holy Word,
Knowing with assurance we shall be united again.

May God embrace you with His love,
Give you grace and solace from above.
May you feel His comfort while in deep sorrow,
And know He is with you during this hour.

Through salvation we soar to a greater height,
For we walk by faith, not by sight.
His Holy Word to us is our covenant,
And His promises to us are all permanent.

Confidence in God's Word validates our hope,
For God heals the heart and soothes the soul.
He miraculously comforts and makes us whole,
And removes our nightmare as He gently consoles.

May you be blessed and be of good courage,
And receive His peace that surpasses all understanding.
Always know you are never alone,
He upholds you and He will make you strong.

Place in Him your unwavering trust,
Rely upon Him and He will give you rest.
He loves you and will carry you through,
He will surely sustain and restore you.

Our future is brighter than our present,
Remain in prayer and stay in His presence.
For now, we comfort one another with charity,
Until we reside with Him in the celestial city.

The Ocean

The ocean's mesmerizing magnificence,
Is blissful and calming,
And its inspiring elegance,
Is tranquil and charming.

The ocean's striking grandeur,
Is exhilarating and enchanting,
While its superb presence,
Is comforting and commanding.

The ocean's majestic beauty,
Is seductive and alluring,
And its rhythmic waves,
Are soothing and sedating.

The ocean's great splendor,
Is picturesque and spectacular,
And it evokes a peace,
That is serenely heavenly.

The ocean's gorgeous ambiance,
Is captivating and peaceful,
And its engrossing grace,
Is relaxing and delightful.

The ocean's wondrous view,
Is pleasantly refreshing,
While its enticing loveliness,
Is brilliantly radiating.

The ocean glistens,
Displaying the sky's reflection,
As its white waves gently sway,
Carrying ones cares far away.

Looking For Mister Right

This I ask You everyday,
Lord, send him soon, I pray.
Let his love be tender and true,
Let him love me and love You.

May his integrity be second to none,
May our hearts bond as if we were one.
May he have a radiant warmth,
May he be romantic and lots of fun.

Let him be sincerely dedicated,
Let him definitely be educated.
Let his intelligence be intriguing,
Let his conversations be interesting.

If he is handsome that wouldn't hurt,
High morals would be icing on the cake.
If he is thoughtful and kind,
That would be enjoyable all the time.

May he bring me flowers on a whim,
Knowing how much I love them.
May he give me perfume that's especially mine,
With notes from him that make me smile.

Let his heart be warm and genuine,
Let him be a wonderful companion.
May our love be as healthy as our lives,
May we become husband and wife.

Lord, this I ask You everyday,
Let us meet without delay.
If it is Your will, I pray,
May You answer this prayer today.

Amazing Autumn

Tree leaves are changing to amazing colors,
Red, orange, and golden tell us it is autumn.
Picturesque enough to be recorded on camera,
These sights would make a beautiful calendar.

The autumn days grow cooler and much shorter,
We forget not long ago the days were much warmer.
People are taking brisk walks in the cooler weather,
Admiring the scenery before they prepare for Winter.

The air is quite crisp and most refreshing,
Birds are soaring South as enthusiasts are watching.
Hunters are resuming their woodland hunting,
Farmers diligently doing apple orchard picking.

Parents are raking yards as children are playing,
Kids falling into mounds of leaves as they are romping.
Neighbors visiting fishing streams before they are frozen,
Catching large tasty pink salmon by the dozen.

Fireplaces are warming and chimneys smoking,
Kids waiting excitedly as their marshmallows are roasting.
Couples snuggling lovingly near fireplaces that are roaring,
Enjoying the ambiance of a setting that is heartwarming.

Children are getting ready to return to school,
Buying necessary supplies is the usual rule.
College students preparing for classes to resume,
Gearing up for the educational challenges that loom.

Autumn is such a beautiful amazing season,
We look forward to it for a multiplicity of reasons.
Implicitly, autumn ushers in Halloween and Thanksgiving,
Fortunate are we to share in this style of living.

The Enlistment

He has enlisted at the recruitment station,
Saying he wants to go fight for our nation.
Oh, what pain and emotional cost,
All because his presence will be lost.

What can I do in his long absence,
Hope for his return to come faster.
I'll miss the sound of his hardy laughter,
Long for his smile as he listens to me chatter.

I already dread the day of his departure,
Each day I am with him, I will treasure.
If only the days would grow much longer,
And the weeks move quite a bit slower.

His leaving will place my life on pause,
How can I move when my heart has stalled?
My world has suddenly turned upside down,
I am feeling helpless to turn it around.

He is such a warm remarkable person,
And lights up a room with his very presence.
He is the sunshine in my wonderful life,
And he is the spark that makes me smile.

He has such a calm serene essence,
Touching his life has been my blessing.
The thought of his untimely leaving,
Makes me wish that I were dreaming.

Knowing I must be strong for his sake,
I will certainly put on my best face.
Smiling as the tears are choking in my throat,
I will bid him farewell as he boards the boat.

Grandpa's Birthday Bash

Sending invitations for Grandpa's birthday bash,
Hoping the guest won't, "Let the cat out of the bag."
Working feverishly to complete all the decorations,
To surprise Grandpa at his special celebration.

Grandpa came on a ruse to watch his hockey team play,
Entering the house, we shouted, "Happy Birthday!"
He is somewhat stunned and obviously very surprised,
Observing the scene, he flashes his remarkable smile.

Grandpa has accumulated quite a brood,
Children with spouses, and hordes of grandchildren.
Old friends, neighbors, and buddies from far away,
All coming to wish Grandpa the very best birthday.

Grandma has helped prepare quite a feast,
A delicious potluck buffet fit for a king.
Decorations, party hats, and balloons are everywhere,
Music, gaiety, and laughter in this jovial atmosphere.

Grandpa has his favorite birthday dessert,
A huge three layer strawberry cream cake.
It's so delicious it melts in your mouth,
Like eating a soft sweet edible cloud.

Grandpa has mounds of wonderful presents,
Slippers, fishing rods, and hunting jackets.
He unwraps gifts from shirts to warm sweaters,
Pausing to thank each one as cameras are flashing.

Grandpa receives loads of hugs and kisses,
As everyone gives him their best wishes.
Grandpa had quite a celebratory birthday bash,
We all wish this day would always last!

The Proposal

I must ask this fervent question,
Will you be my lifetime companion?
I ask you to become my wife,
And share with me the rest of my life?

I promise to dedicate my life to you,
To have integrity and always be true.
I adore you and surrender my emotions,
And promise you my lifelong devotion.

I love you and cherish your love,
Our uniting has been guided from above.
Your presence is my marvelous blessing,
Your love I will always treasure.

My adoration for you only will always remain,
My honesty and faithfulness, I truly affirm.
I give you my heart without reservation,
I will cleave to you with enraptured affection.

I am enthralled by your beauty and gracefulness,
And fascinated by your warmth and genuineness.
I am enchanted with your charm and loveliness,
And desirous of your lasting companionship.

I am sincerely captivated by your presence,
With confidence, we were meant for each other.
I entrust my endearing love to you forever,
With certainty, we were destined to be together.

I offer this ring as my commitment,
And I pledge my love to you unconditionally.
I will cherish you for the rest of my life,
If you will accept my ring and become my wife.

My Best Friend

We thoroughly enjoy each other genuinely,
Sharing our lives as if we were family.
Talking on the phone to one another daily,
Ever relishing in each other's company.

Listening to one another's joys and frustrations,
Supporting each other regardless to the situations.
Communicating loquaciously as if it were catharsis,
All because we are avid chatter enthusiasts.

Telling each other what enhances their attributes,
Even if it means a friendly squabble will pursue.
Enlightening one another about the very best sales,
Shopping together sometimes until night prevails.

Listening intensely to one another's problems,
Investing emotions and insight to help solve them.
Always available to give a helping hand,
We will uphold each other through thick and thin.

Hoping soon to meet our significant others,
Keeping our spirits high through joy and laughter.
Reveling in hilarious stories from our past,
Sharing humorous anecdotes from our parents.

Our personalities have such compatible harmony,
We discuss everything from our careers to the economy.
Happily we cherish our reciprocal friendship,
It is such a positive element along life's trip.

Although our home visits are usually very few,
There is the greatest of respect between us two.
It is most comforting to have a best friend,
One who will stand with me to the very end.

Only A Season

Everyone has dark times,
Hardships, suffering, and tribulations.
These may be the preparations,
For great life transitions.
Things come for a reason,
And last for only a season.

Dark times have a purpose,
Building character and developing the person.
Do not become overwhelmed,
If the future appears bleak and dim.
Things come for a reason,
And last for only a season.

Dark times train the person,
From raising children to leading nations.
Obstacles serve as elevations,
Experiences build strong foundations.
Things come for a reason,
And last for only a season.

Dark times translate afflictions,
Into growth under hard conditions.
Exploring in-depth introspections,
May give one new directions.
Things come for a reason,
And last for only a season.

Dark times develop courage,
Under difficult circumstances.
Life's greatest challenges,
Discover abilities and talents.
Things come for a reason,
And last for only a season.

Dark times cultivate competence,
Experiences bring confidence.
Conditions forged by complexities,
Channeled into opportunities.
Things come for a reason,
And last for only a season.

Dark times come to an end,
A new day extends.
Ones learning is shared,
Constructive occasions are everywhere.
Things come for a reason,
And last for only a season.

Lovers Meet Again

Hi there, it is great to see you,
My, you still look good.
This is such a pleasant surprise,
I could hardly believe my eyes.

How are things going with you,
Evidently, everything is quite good.
Oh, how I have longed for this day,
I am astonished, what can I say!

Will you join me and have a seat,
We can talk over a cup of tea.
I have thought of you and longed for you often,
And sorely missed you as my companion.

Our meeting is truly my blessing,
This is that for which I have been praying.
I have desired to see your lovely face,
Hoped to see you in crowds and in various places.

How I wish we had never parted,
Life without you is like a book without writing.
You are the necessary lyrics for my life,
It is you that make me feel vibrant and alive.

Can we renew our love once again,
And resume the pleasures that we had.
I do hope we will give our hearts a chance,
And let our love blossom into a romance.

I still love you and I always will,
My love has not changed despite the vacant years.
If anything, the time has increased my passion,
I know we will have a life filled with happiness!

Spa Enchantment

Reclining and reflecting on a spa supreme,
An exquisitely beautiful quite elegant suite.
Luxurious and charming bath amenities,
Gorgeously decorated for superb tranquility.

Adorably embellished lovely spa facilities,
Aqua blue water swirling soothingly.
Silkened bath gels enriched and refreshing,
Immense effervesce with cloud magnificence.

Crystal sconces dimmed to reflect twilight,
Luxurious chandeliers twinkling as starlight.
Gleaming candlelight dazzling enchantingly,
A glowing hue flickering artistically.

Beautiful colorful roses arranged lavishly,
Accents of "baby breath" enhancing angelically.
Delicate floral aroma wonderfully captivating,
A lovely fragrance delightfully lingering.

Music playing softly sedating and serene,
Melodies floating throughout this amazing suite.
Chocolate-dipped-strawberries deliciously scrumptious,
Sipping tasteful beverages in crystal goblets.

Delightfully soothing and marvelously rejuvenating,
Pleasantly calming and splendidly reinvigorating.
Feeling satiny smooth and ravishly cozy,
Blissfully renewed and superbly mellow.

Sublimely enthralled with this grandeur spa,
Enraptured with its splendor and glorious aura.
With hopeful dreams and a devised strategy,
Perhaps someday it may become my reality.

It's My Fault, Not His

His blows sent me reeling,
The children are screaming.
If I could just do things right,
Because it's my fault, not his.

His words are chilling,
The pain sends me cringing.
If I could just do things right,
Because it's my fault, not his.

The money he is spending,
His addiction is descending.
If I could just do things right,
Because it's my fault, not his.

His stumbling is embarrassing,
The stench is revealing.
If I could just do things right,
Because it's my fault, not his.

He says I'm disgusting,
So his life is failing.
If I could just do things right,
Because it's my fault, not his.

This life is draining,
But I'm not complaining.
If I could just do things right,
Because it's my fault, not his.

He will change, if I just hold tight,
The officials said, I have rights.
But, how can I resolve this plight,
Because it's my fault, not his.

The Backyard Barbeque

The coals are hot in the barbeque pit,
The hickory wood is a great complement.
The aroma is floating through the neighborhood,
Letting the neighbors know we are cooking good.

Ribs and chicken are slowly smoked,
So the cook can avidly boast.
Tender and tasty is his barbeque,
The flavor is embedded through and through.

Tubs of tall cold drinks are on ice,
To quench the thirst and make things nice.
Hamburgers and hotdogs are made in a batch,
Kids are munching on them as a snack.

The cob corn and potato salad are perfect,
The meaty baked beans are some of the best.
The steaks and green salad surpass their test,
Peach cobbler and ice cream round out the rest.

The water is splashing in the aqua blue pool,
Children are floating and swimming to stay cool.
Acrobatic diving maneuvers are going strong,
Everyone's yelling for their favorite actions.

Some are reclining on the pool deck,
Sunbathing comfortably just to relax.
Many are playing games, others chatting together,
Music is playing, everyone's enjoying each other.

The cook is clanging his triangular chime,
Calling, "Come and get it, everything's done."
This barbeque feast is such a great delight,
The cook's getting accolades to the heights!

I've Got To Have Her

When my eyes laid upon her,
My heart bonded with her eternally.
My soul was entwined until the end of time,
I've got to make her mine.

I've got to have her; she's my destiny,
Without her my life is incomplete.
My passion for her is unquenchable,
The love in my heart is immeasurable.

Her exotic beauty is mesmerizing,
Her gorgeous eyes are fascinating.
Her luminous skin and flowing hair,
She is enchanting beyond compare.

She is the nucleus of my life,
Her companionship is sublime.
Our compatibility is uniquely divine,
I beseeched her to join me as my wife.

Accept this ring as our loving engagement,
Receive my love as a lifetime commitment.
Our wedding bliss was most magnificent,
Our marriage is ever a nuptial entrustment.

The passion of our love is ecstasy,
The sharing of our lives is enchanting.
The mother of my children most gratifying,
I'm gratefully enthralled for our uniting.

When my eyes laid upon her,
My heart bonded with her eternally.
My soul was entwined until the end of time,
I had to make her mine.

United We Stand

America, strong united and free,
From Alaska to the Florida Keys.
Thru Hawaii's shores to the Atlantic sands,
Abundantly blessed; united we stand.

Magnanimously grateful living our dreams,
Constantly thankful for all our means.
Exceedingly appreciative for abundance achieved,
Acutely cognizant of magnificent blessings received.

Profoundly proud of our military corps,
Superbly protecting our homeland shores.
Bountifully supporting their valiant stance,
Abundantly blessed; united we stand.

Tenaciously striving for accomplishments acquired,
Persistently pursuing acquisitions desired.
Launching conquest toward ventures unknown,
Obtaining success through perseverance renown.

Conquering horizons formidable to some,
Challenging obstructions regardless the forms.
Sincerely embracing this great beautiful land,
Abundantly blessed; united we stand.

Freely making our political choices,
Selecting leaders through electoral voices.
Fervently bonding through disasters plights,
Fearlessly defending our nation's rights.

America, strong and majestically enhanced,
Awesomely engraciated by God's own hands.
Graciously sharing wherever we can,
Abundantly blessed; united we stand.

Winter's Bliss

Listening to the pitter-patter of rain,
Splashing rhythmically on the window pane.
Slipping softly into my bubble bathtub,
Nibbling on a dish of nut-filled fudge.

Waffling aroma of warm gingerbread,
Munching this treat while still in bed.
Sipping hot chocolate from my special mug,
Humming along with my favorite songs.

Skating blissfully on the frozen pond,
Swaying merrily and having fun.
Whisking breeze flowing through my hair,
Enjoying the scenery while skating as a pair.

Feeling the splendor of drifting snowflakes,
Brushing ever gently upon my face.
Twirling playfully with outstretched arms,
Floating snow flurries are so much fun.

Gliding down fluffy powdery ski slopes,
Swooping smoothly through mounds of snow.
Pausing to watch herds of galloping antelopes,
Leaping gracefully as if they float.

Browsing through my Winter magazines,
Glancing at the architecture and cuisine.
Snuggling under my warm cozy afghan,
Thinking what a month this has been.

Embracing the wonders of Winter's bliss,
Wishing it could always be like this.
Drifting into a peaceful slumberland,
Dreaming that Winter is about to begin.

The Wedding

You are cordially invited,
To our fanciful dream wedding.
It will be laced with glamour,
To be held in a fairytale manner.

We extend our warmest hospitality,
Requesting your presence at our cathedral chapel.
May you witness our sacred ceremony,
As we exchange our vows at the altar.

My beautiful bride floating angelically down the aisle,
Appearing as a princess in a gown elegantly divine;
Embellished lavishly with crystals, beads, and pearls,
And the chapel length train of a fantasy world.

I take you to be my lawfully wedded wife,
To have and to hold for my entire life.
With this ring I thee wed, in elation,
I pledge my love and lifetime devotion.

The ballroom reception is in exquisite decorum,
Spectacularly decorated in satin with amazing flowers.
The cuisine is regal and impeccably presented,
An extravagant six course superb dinner.

Our delicious five tier cake is decorated artistically,
Sculptured with flowers in Italian cream icing.
Feeling ecstatic slicing into its cascading artistry,
We present each other this delectable delicacy.

Blissfully celebrating our wedding dance,
Gliding magically as though in fantasy land.
Bidding farewell as our carriage is drawn,
As doves soar symbolizing peace for our new horizons.

Thanksgiving At Grandma's

Thanksgiving dinner is in Grandma's hands,
She's planning and cooking days in advance.
She knows everyone's favorite requests,
We all know her food will be the best.

Grandma's food has that southern touch,
She can pinch and dash, but not too much.
She has old recipes, but not written down,
Sharing these nuggets as we stand around.

Grandma roasts her juicy turkey golden brown,
It's picture perfect and melts in the mouth.
She's a master at savory turkey stuffing,
We love her mean-greens and cornbread muffins.

Grandma's cooking beats a master chef's,
Her festive holiday table's dressed to impress.
She uses her fine china and crystal stemware,
Bouquets of handpicked flowers she grew herself.

Grandma bakes the best homemade desserts,
She serves sweet potato pies and butter cakes.
Her deep-dish peach cobbler will make you moan,
It will cause you to smile all the way home.

Grandma's house is filled with festive cheer,
Babies, grandchildren, and all those dear.
Everyone has traveled from near and far,
We must be with Grandma because she's the star.

Grandma tucks lots of love into each dish,
She prepares everyone's Thanksgiving wish.
We love all of Grandma's harvest feast abound,
But we're most thankful that Grandma's still around!

Compulsions

The crap tables are humming,
The blackjack is jamming,
The roulette wheels are spinning,
The slot machines are ringing,
The bank accounts are empty!

The beer is nothing,
The gin is not harming,
The bourbon just gives a buzz,
The whiskey takes off the edge,
The rationalizations are building up!

The stores are irresistible,
The merchandise is abundant,
The credit cards are delinquent,
The pain is driving me insane,
The obsession is running amok!

The football, I must watch,
The baseball is my favorite,
The basketball, I have to follow,
The boxing, I can't let go,
The family has moved next door!

I ate enough, but the food is great,
I will just snack, it won't hurt,
I'm not hungry, but I must eat something,
I know I'm stuffed, but I'm just munching,
The excuses I constantly make-up!

The diet pills, I must be slim,
The sedatives, I can't part with them,
The pain pills, I can't give up,
The tranquilizers, I need to relax,
The justifications are growing thin!

The depression, I'm fighting,
The panic is frightening,
The life is unraveling,
The compulsions are rescinding,
But who am I fooling?

Missed Opportunities

You married the best woman you ever had,
You should have worked for your marriage to last.
Instead you worked at relentless misuse,
By inflicting mental, emotional, and verbal abuse.

You did not value your spousal jewel,
You should have cherished her with great morals.
Instead you philandered with every woman you could,
By constantly committing adultery frivolously, as a fool.

You did not treasure your dedicated wife,
You should have joined her in working for a better life.
Instead you followed a dreadful path of blight,
By alcoholism and using illicit drugs to the heights.

You did not serve as a decent honorable father,
You should have been your children's positive role model.
Instead you introduced them to your despicable lifestyle,
By teaching them to consume things that were most reviled.

You did not demonstrate family leadership traditions,
You should have exemplified integrity and strong ambitions.
Instead you were incompatible in family life,
By being devoid of providing necessary social delights.

You did not think your true-self would ever be revealed,
You should have known no one has an impenetrable shield.
Instead you thought you could live a life of disguise,
By what you called, "Keeping your fingers in others' eyes."

You did not think your game would come to an end,
You should have known you would reap the whirlwind.
Although you thought your world was shatterproof,
Your missed opportunities resulted in deplorable self-abuse.

Spring Is Here

The days are bright warm and sunny,
Flowers arrayed in variegated beauty.
The grass is as colorful as bluegreen carpets,
Cherry trees adorned in floral blossoms.

Meadows are saturated with wild flowers,
Fields bursting in billows of brilliant colors.
Bees busily collecting juicy sweet nectar,
Pollinating flowers to make the honey better.

The placid deep blue lake is gently rippling,
A perfectly picturesque site for those fishing.
Beautiful butterflies are gracefully swooping,
Birds chirping musically as they are soaring.

Blankets spread on the grass in clusters,
Picnic baskets filled with banquet lunches.
Couples watching as toddlers scamper,
Kids hopping in sacks racing to be winners.

Marinas laden with yachts and motorboats,
Gliding in scenic blue waters as they float.
Baseball games played in crowded stadiums,
Fans buoyantly cheering for their players.

Amusement parks swarmed with excited visitors,
Enjoying rides, water slides, and roller coasters.
NASCAR races packed with dedicated loyal fans,
Drivers competing to be in the winner's stand.

Excitement and fun during the long spring days,
Outside activities are enjoyed in various ways.
Picnics, barbeques, and theme park fun,
Swim parties, hiking, there is something for everyone!

The Honeymoon

We entered our opulently grandeur honeymoon suite,
It was palatial with an essence most unique.
He adoringly looked into my eyes saying, "You are my wife."
I lovingly responded, "I'm yours for the rest of my life."

We awoke to the sun shining brightly into our room,
Reminiscing, we felt our wedding was over too soon.
The valet served a sumptuous breakfast quite gourmet,
As we fed each other, we planned the rest of our day.

We sailed on pristine waters serene and aqua blue,
Landing on a beautiful island was a dream come true.
We knew our honeymoon would be like a fairytale,
Enjoying this wonderful bliss seemed like another world.

Scuba diving we watched colorful fish glistening in the sun,
We explored coral reefs amazed at how they were done.
Returning to the beach, we reclined on the warm white sand,
Relaxing, we genuinely enjoyed this quaint marvelous land.

Sublimely we meandered through lush tropical gardens,
Mesmerized with the splendor of the trees, plants, and flowers.
Enthralled in these spectacularly gorgeous living murals,
Wishing we could remain among the lovely scents of floral.

Dining in a superbly enchanting ambiance,
Adoration for the exquisite cuisine that was fabulous.
Delighting in the majestic scene as candles twinkled as starlight,
Lovingly holding hands as we shared this glorious night.

Our honeymoon was the most blissful experience of our lives,
We enjoyed precious enchantments we hold for a lifetime.
The pleasures that we shared will always be treasured,
We embrace the wonderment of starting our new life together.

Being Your Best

If I cannot be a glorious singer,
Let me be a wonderful writer.
If I cannot paint beautiful artistry,
Let me be a superior counselor.

If I cannot be a talented musician,
Let me be a skillful technician.
If I cannot be a meticulous pharmacist,
Let me be an inventive scientist.

If I cannot be a college professor,
Let me be a great building contractor.
If I cannot be a medical physician,
Let me be an outstanding politician.

If I cannot be a memorable actor,
Let me be a superbly gifted dancer.
If I cannot be a magnanimous architect,
Let me be a magnificent culinary chef.

If I cannot be a stupendous engineer,
Let me be an ingenious manufacture.
If I cannot be an awesome teacher,
Let me be a renowned fashion designer.

If I cannot be an outstanding lawyer,
Let me be a splendid police officer.
If I cannot be a professional athlete,
Let me be an exceptional editor-in-chief.

There are opportunities from the apex to the zenith,
You can have careers from an analyst to a zoologist.
Everyone can reach their potentials and horizons,
By striving tenaciously to achieve their career ambitions.

Convicted Without A Charge

Accused by a fallacy,
Stripped by the law,
Suffering injustice,
Though there was no flaw.

Without a trial,
With no jury deployed,
Accusations assail,
Convicted without a charge.

Charged by the media,
Condemned by tabloids,
Falsehoods run rapid,
Though facts are void.

Without a trial,
With no jury deployed,
Accusations assail,
Convicted without a charge.

Truth forfeited,
Lifestyle misunderstood,
Suffering indignities,
A nightmare for sure!

Without a trial,
With no jury deployed,
Accusations assail,
Convicted without a charge.

Denounced and judged,
Career almost destroyed,
With life derailed,
Convicted without a charge!

Retirement

No more setting clock alarms,
No more getting up at the crack of dawn.
No more rushing and dressing frantically,
No more fighting the morning traffic.

No more making those long slow commutes,
Coming in late having to make an excuse.
No more diabolical workplace politics,
Employee gossip and malicious tactics.

No more annual employee evaluations,
Hoping to receive a good rating.
No more working for the dollar,
Answering to the person with the white collar.

When I am through resting and sleeping,
I will get in my boat and go sailing.
When I finish leisurely gardening,
I will get my pole and go fishing.

When I am through reading pleasurable books,
I will go find something delicious to cook.
When I feel I need to go and roam,
I will take a vacation in my mobile home.

When I am through exercising to stay thin,
I will jump in my pool and take a swim.
When I feel I want another new car,
I will go to the showroom and buy a sports Jaguar.

When I am through shopping for recreation,
I will get with friends and enjoy pure elation.
When I think of the workplace drama,
I will turn over and drift asleep calmly.

The Introduction

Hello, I've been admiring you,
I saw you from across the room.
May I say you have exotic beauty,
You are stunning and quite unusual.

Do you mind if I have a seat,
I'm pleased we had a chance to meet.
May I get you anything,
Something from the buffet or a fresh drink?

Do you like the song that's playing,
May I ask you for this dance?
You dance so light and smooth,
And may I say, I love your perfume.

I'm glad I came to this party,
For sometime, I have socialized rarely.
Do you mind if we step onto the veranda,
To get some air and talk with more candor.

I hope you won't think I'm too inquisitive,
But I do hope you are available.
I have not been on a date in ages,
I've been on a long hiatus.

Here is the number to my home phone,
It would be my pleasure for you to call.
Perhaps soon I can take you to lunch,
Or you can join me for Sunday brunch.

This evening has been such a delight,
All because I met you tonight.
If you are feeling the excitement that I do,
I hope this is the beginning for us two.

Christmas Season

Christmas season is excitedly in the air,
Yuletide adornments are everywhere.
Noel songs serenading holiday shoppers,
Boulevards decked with festive ornaments.

Homes decorated from chimneys to yards,
Christmas lights dancing in the dark.
Reindeers and snowmen on scenic lawns,
Yuletide wreaths affixed to embellished doors.

Sending Christmas cards near and far,
Tucking in photos we love to share.
Jotting notes to those we hold dear,
Wishing everyone happiness and cheer.

Using Internet shopping resources,
Hoping the gifts are the right choices.
Stashing the wealth of children's toys,
Wrapping all of this Christmas joy.

Christmas trees lavish with decorations,
Gifts abundant causing great jubilation.
Children scampering to open presents,
Gleeful with excitement and expectation.

Giving thanks for these great blessings,
Dining on the most scrumptious dinners.
Sharing all these holiday festivities,
Enjoying wonderful friends and families.

What a joyous blessed Christmas season,
What a marvelous Christian day of rejoicing.
The birth of Christ is the reason for the celebration,
With gratefulness we enjoy this day in exaltation.

Mother, Mom, Love

My mother, my mom is my best friend,
She will stand with me to the end.
When I reminisce of one with delight,
It is her image that comes into sight.

When untold burdens cause me despair,
She cradles my head and strokes my hair.
When my life appears to be in disrepair,
She holds me close and says God is there.

She has comfort in her touch,
She has insight that I trust.
She has words of wisdom that I cherish,
She has a presence of peace that I treasure.

My mother, my mom will always be,
She lives in my child and she lives in me.
She is God's precious gift from above,
She is mother; she is mom; she is love.

When life presents uncertain choices,
She poses questions and I perceive answers.
When I share with her delicate secrets,
She listens attentively without judgments.

When I need someone to genuinely care,
She holds me up in fervent prayer.
When I share laughter from the heart,
She has given me the origin of this joy.

My mother, my mom will always be,
She lives in my child and she lives in me.
She is God's precious gift from above,
She is mother; she is mom; she is love.

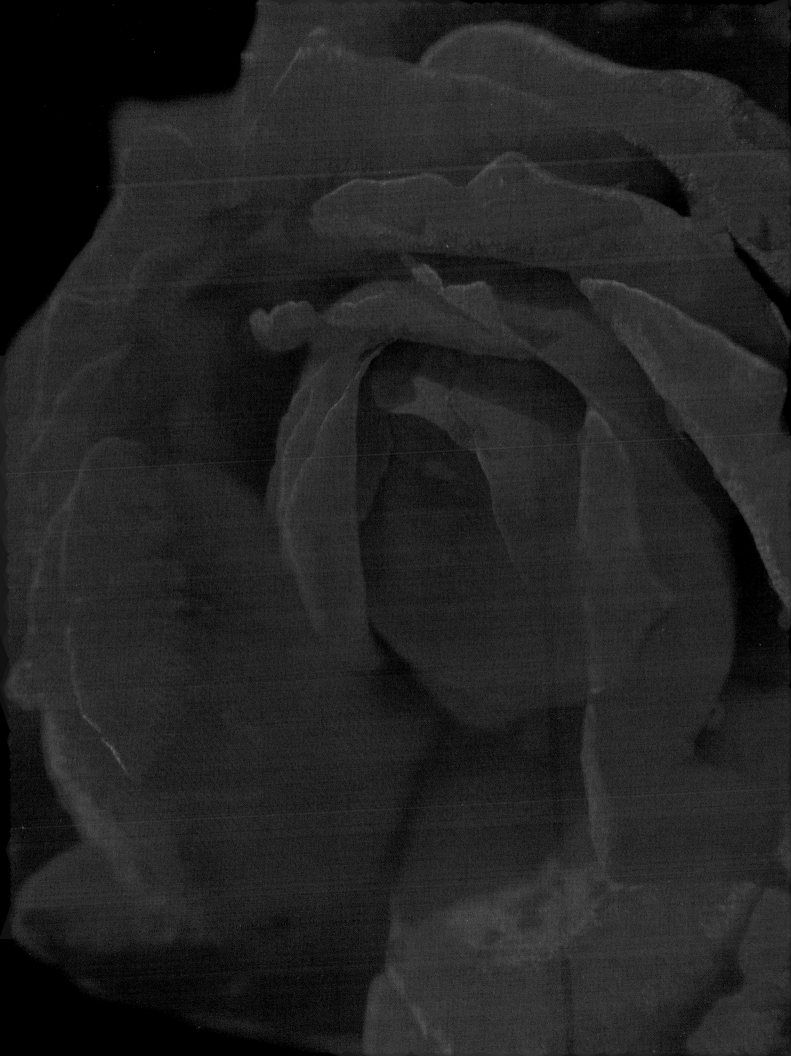

Love

Love is an internal companion,
It warms the heart,
And comforts tenderly.
It will be with us for eternity.

Love is deeper than the grave,
And deeper than the sea.
Love is with us constantly,
It will last an eternity.

Love is ever present,
And it knows no boundaries.
Love is a gift to the world,
It will live on in eternity.

Love is giving freely,
And it demonstrates charity.
Love is sharing with others,
For our works will last eternally.

Love is longsuffering,
And it extends helping hands.
Love shows concern for others,
It will be our reward eternally.

Love consists of two commandments,
To love God and to love each other.
Love lives on perpetually,
It goes with us to eternity.

Love is a universal force,
It bonds heaven to the earth.
Love is ever wondrous,
It ushers us into eternity.

Karma The Mega Bummer

When you are having that sordid affair,
Thinking no one will ever be aware,
Things done in the dark do come to the light,
God is watching and records every sight.

Payday someday according to your works,
Payday is coming and it's your hell on earth.
Karma is a mega bummer and it has no pity,
Karma will make you regret you ever did it!

When you plan to destroy someone's employment,
Devising devious acts for your enjoyment.
Concocting fallacies reported to the board,
Remember, "Vengeance is mine," says the Lord.

When you try to control someone with mental abuse,
Destroying anyone emotionally, there is no excuse.
Are you assuming that you have supremacy,
You must be informed that only God is Deity.

Payday someday according to your works,
Payday is coming and it's your hell on earth.
Karma is a mega bummer and it has no pity,
Karma will make you regret you ever did it!

When you usurp others financial identity,
You are destroying their entire fiscal viability.
Negatively impacting someone's life and dignity,
You will definitely pay whether here or in eternity.

When you are exposed you shield with major lies,
Hoping your fabrications will be a sufficient disguise.
Remember, what is done in the dark does come to the light,
Karma is so effective sometimes it shortens ones life!

He Is A Dandy

Reveling in clubs past midnight,
Guzzling cocktails left and right,
Doing whatever he fancies,
He is a dandy.

Buzzing nothings in ladies ears,
Saying what they want to hear,
Pretending to be classy,
He is a dandy.

Racing chums on motorbikes,
Throwing dust until out of sight,
Flipping whirlys is manly,
He is a dandy.

Skirmishing in barroom brawls,
Having a little fun that's all,
Chugging mugs of brandy,
He is a dandy.

Chasing women for the sport,
Leaving lovers in every port,
Taking frightening chances,
He is a dandy.

Dragging through boulevard strips,
Going to jail on some trips,
Losing a rear end chassis,
He is a dandy.

Resting in his hospital bed,
Rubbing the gauze on his head,
Needing finances badly,
He is a dandy!

Remembering

Remembering when we first met,
Enjoying the splendor of our budding romance.
Remembering the joy you brought into my life,
Glowing when you took me to be your wife.

Remembering when we were newlyweds,
Basking in the deep passion we shared.
Remembering your warm loving embrace,
Believing I was the most fortunate woman on earth.

Remembering setting up our first house,
Learning of each other's diverse styles.
Remembering when we were expecting our child,
Planning life changes as our excitement ran wild.

Remembering the struggles that brought growth,
Holding on though we were tossed to-and-fro.
Remembering when we moved to another city,
Moving on as we scaled life's great ladder.

Remembering the excitement of your home arrivals,
Coming home after a workday made our lives brighter.
Remembering the daily fun and laughter,
Relishing in our love as we grew closer.

Remembering how our lives became fused,
Feeling no longer individuals, but one unit.
Remembering always sleeping in your arms,
Loving the pleasure of your comfort and warmth.

Remembering how we made family traditions,
Meeting challenges and adjusting to life transitions.
Remembering how our lives united through destiny,
Knowing that our love will last eternally.

Still, The Child Cries

His achievements are exceptional,
His accomplishments are comparable.
He's acquired a suave mystique,
While brushing kisses on women's cheeks.
Still, the child cries.

He's derived a life of ease,
He's even attained professional degrees.
He cruises comfortably in his Mercedes,
He romances women as a tease.
Still, the child cries.

He's traveled the world,
He's conquered multiple girls.
His words are fluid and smooth,
Manipulation is his usual tool.
Still, the child cries.

He thought with much success,
The inner-man would have inner-rest.
His child, a significant part,
Echoing past words, chilling his heart.
Still, the child cries.

His child is the inner-man,
Feeling discomfort he does not understand.
He's searching for solace and safety,
He's seeking in all the wrong places.
Still, the child cries.

He's been battered and abused,
He's suffered childhood misuse.
He's vowed his life would be reversed,
His past is repeated, as if rehearsed.
Still, the child cries.

Unconditional love extends her hand,
Genuine throughout his life span.
Apprehension delays his clasp,
The child must learn to trust.
Gently, gently, the child's cries are dried.

Love At First Sight

When I first looked into your face,
My voice remained politely reserved.
Since my legs had begun weakening,
I left your presence to avoid collapsing.

I was actually falling in love with you,
But what was I suppose to do?
I decided to stay out of your presence,
To avoid doing something embarrassing.

How could I have possibly known,
You had fallen in love with me too?
Destiny had played its wondrous hand,
A phone call placed as if it were planned.

We connected as if it were fate,
You asked me on our first date.
Before that wonderful night was through,
You embraced me and sealed our future.

We became inseparable bonding intuitively,
And we dated each other exclusively.
We were complete in our world,
I was enthralled to be your girl.

Miraculously this was a dream come true,
I had a magnetic passion for you.
We were so perfectly compatible,
A more devoted couple rarely happened.

In your arms was my bliss,
The rest of the world, I did not miss.
Our deep love did not falter,
And it led us to the wedding altar.

New Year's Celebration

Preparing for the New Year's celebration,
Arranging all the festive decorations.
Planning for the best of entertainment,
Enjoying friends in splendid merriment.

Caterers extending exquisite hospitality,
Fountains flowing with tasteful refreshments.
Buffets laden with delectable delicacies,
Assortments of delicious gourmet pastries.

Ecstatic jubilation for another year,
Sharing our exuberance with those dear.
Magical festivity in the glitter and glamour,
Joyous gaiety of the party revelers.

Bands buoyantly playing rhythmic tunes,
Vocalist jovially singing vivacious songs.
Balloons cascading on ballroom crowds,
Partygoers dancing until the break of dawn.

City squares jammed with exuberant partiers,
Zealously frolicking in the New Year's Eve splendor.
Gleefully relishing in the holiday exhilaration,
Anticipating the New Year with enthusiastic elation.

The New Year's ball dropping in Times Square,
Jubilant excitement is building everywhere.
Fireworks are bursting colorfully in the air,
We are counting down to the splendid New Year.

Congratulatory kisses and good cheer,
Joyfulness and happiness beyond compare.
Amazement and thankfulness everyone's here,
Wishing all a very prosperous New Year!

The Other Woman

Woe is me, he uses as his tear jerking line,
He has nothing in common with his wife.
She's so cold they sleep in separate rooms,
Except for the children, he would be leaving soon.

He tells you how he's sorely abused,
So unhappy he needs to be soothed.
He's so glad he has finally met you,
He forgot to tell you, you're being used.

He strokes you with passionate lies,
Claiming you make him feel so alive.
He needs you to always be there,
Most likely he's having another affair.

He's attending elegant dinners and gala parties,
Proudly escorting his Mrs. as his partner.
You're usually staying home all alone,
Wishing he would call you on the phone.

His holidays are always most restricted,
Nights and weekends are quite limited.
Though he can't bring you to the light,
To family and friends he's upright.

Sporadic times do you and he share,
Sometimes saying he's unable to appear.
Never knowing when he will be free,
Desperately clinging to his feeble fallacies.

Hidden fervor is not worth the plight,
There is no contentment because it's not right.
He's making excuse and repeatedly rationalizing,
While your misguided life feels demoralizing.

Relaxation

Long leisure drives,
On Sunday afternoons,
Clears ones mind,
As it relaxes and soothes.

Bicycling on riding trails,
Is exceptionally revitalizing,
And this energizing motion,
Is exceedingly rejuvenating.

Weekend mountain climbs,
Ascending to new heights,
Are spectacular excursions,
And exhilarating to the person.

Swimming and splashing,
In the nearest pool,
Are body enhancing,
And mentally refreshing.

Long country hikes,
Passing fields and pastures,
Listening to sounds of animals,
Bonds ones spirit with nature.

Jogging through the neighborhood,
Passing familiar locations,
Is stimulating and invigorating,
And an enlivening avocation.

Quiet relaxing beach walks,
Listening to ocean waves,
Elevates one internally,
To a higher plane.

The Wedding Anniversary

We will celebrate the day of our wedding,
Expectantly, we will enjoy this exhilarating evening.
He presented me with a gorgeous rose bouquet,
I will place it in the suite where we will stay.

He has made the most impressive reservations,
At a luxurious chateau that was formerly a mansion.
Its ensemble serenades most beautifully,
In an ambiance that makes one feel romantically.

He has requested a celebratory royal dinner,
It makes me feel loved and splendidly regal.
I am gloriously enthralled on this occasion,
It thrills me that he is my beloved companion.

I presented him with an engraved watch to remember,
He gave me a gold necklace with a diamond pendant.
We are wondrously saturated in loving happiness,
The enchantment we feel is quite marvelous.

The soft romantic music is divinely enrapturing,
He is whispering to me lovingly as we are dancing.
The illumination is dimmed and the mood is sensuous,
This magnificent evening has been so fabulous.

Our feelings are reminiscent of our honeymoon,
I am enchanted with him and he feels the same way too.
We are still passionately in love with each other,
Our love grows more wonderful each year we are together.

Our anniversary celebration was sublimely captivating,
The pleasure we shared was gratifying and titillating.
Our mutual adoration gives us joyousness and elation,
We await future anniversaries with great anticipation.

The Equalizer

We are all born equal,
Knowing no prejudice, no bias,
No racism or strife.

We know no divisions,
Whether black, brown,
Red or white.

Then, we expound our difference,
Charging race, religion,
Color or creed.

Therefore, the rejection,
The suffering,
The pain!

Life is but a moment,
Seventy, maybe eighty uncertain years,
With too many unnecessary fears and tears.

Yet, the equalizer draws near,
For one and all,
The equalizer appears.

Death, the equalizer,
Where everyone is equal again,
Everyone is equal again!

- PROGR... MANAGEMENT
- APL FOR MANAGEMENT
- Simulation Using GPSS
- POOLE / FARACH — THE THEORY OF MAGNETIC RESONANCE
- SEEDS — PROGRAMMING RPG / RPG II
- THE GASP IV SIMULATION LANGUAGE
- ARMSTRONG — Modular Programming in COBOL
- Lytel & Buckmaster — abc's of COMPUTERS
- TATHAM — The use of COMPUTERS FOR PROFIT
- PROGRAMMING

Education Is A Tool

Education is a challenge,
To develop skills,
And sharpen talents.
Education is a tool, use it well.

Education is a commitment,
Where success is significant,
And self-motivation is a requisite.
Education is a tool, use it well.

Education is determination,
Which fortifies the person,
To reach ones aspirations.
Education is a tool, use it well.

Education is an expedition,
That expands ones qualifications,
Through scholarly concentration.
Education is a tool, use it well.

Education is knowledge,
Where the mind is challenged,
As objectives are accomplished.
Education is a tool, use it well.

Education is attainable,
With perseverance as an anchor,
Discipline and tenacity as goals.
Education is a tool, use it well.

Education is liberation,
Which can change a nation,
Through dedication and innovations.
Education is a tool, use it well.

Genuine Agony

My discovery of the affair of the two of you,
Caused my soul to weep in agony inconsolably.
My heart grieved at a depth uncontrollable,
The anguish of my tears flowed grippingly sorrowful.

My face was contorted into a silent scream,
This was worse than a horrifying dream.
I had not known the depth of your deception,
Nor did I conceive of such low-life treacherousness.

I was living a virtual terrifying nightmare,
My world had stopped in excruciating despair.
I could have never perceived this happening,
Two people I loved were diabolically deceiving.

My soul was agonizing in the darkest grief,
The pain was immeasurable beyond belief.
My sorrow languished without relief,
I was in the throe of this major catastrophe.

Someone wake me and tell me I was asleep,
This is more pain than I could ever conceive.
How could you do such an abominable thing,
How could you be so heinous and disgusting?

Such gutter-low years of adulterous incest,
Why have you torn my heart within my chest?
You have ripped the cords of my life,
I have never deserved such deceit and strife.

What is so torturous is you are my genuine sibling,
And he is my lawfully most beloved husband.
But God has put this saga to a final rest,
By your tormented lives and premature deaths.

My First Date

I'm so excited,
Oh, the anticipation,
I can't wait!
It's my first date.

What should I wear,
I'm trying to fix this hair,
Will I enjoy it!
It's my first date.

Is this outfit appropriate,
Will we be compatible,
Will we do this again?
It's my first date.

Oh, things are going fine,
The ambiance is beautiful,
The fragrance is delightful.
It's my first date.

The entertainment is quite good,
The conversation is the best,
The time is passing too fast.
It's my first date.

Everything went great!
Should I send a thank you note?
Will the telephone ring soon?
It's my first date.

I remember the very first touch,
My companion is quite a catch.
When I close my eyes today,
I have an instant replay!

Situations

When your finances get funny,
Don't come to me to give you money.
Please go to your selected banker,
That will give me a degree of pleasure.

When you need to borrow a car,
Don't ask me for my newly restored extra.
Please contact your auto rental agency,
That will greatly decrease my anxiety.

When you lose your gas heater's pilot,
Don't call for my husband to come light it.
Please call the gas company for an agent,
That will keep us in good relations.

When you ask me to join you for dinner,
Don't wait for the check to say you left your wallet.
Please say we will pay separately in advance,
That is no problem because I will understand.

When you know my husband is at home,
Don't get dressed up and visit us alone.
Please don't use this gainful ploy,
That play is obvious; your game is to destroy.

When you feel you need to have some fun,
Don't look at my son because he's a juvenile.
Please don't make me get off my rail,
That will certainly cause you to post bail.

When you decide to come to my city,
Don't reside with me because I'm not ready.
Please select the hotel of your choice,
That will give me reason to rejoice.

Lost Love

I loved you from the very start,
But the complexity of life obstructed my choice.
Complications in my life did exist,
If I had trusted my heart, I'd have no regret.

I still love you very passionately,
If I had an opportunity you would see.
I long to see your wonderful loving face,
Wish I could feel your tender embrace.

I love you genuinely and miss you immensely,
If only you could see, I love you unconditionally.
I long to touch your smooth luminous skin,
Desirous to know your love once again.

I sincerely regret the vacant years,
If only I could show you my heart is sincere.
I long to hold you warm and close,
Dreaming of the ecstasy I need the most.

I relish the chance to share with you,
If you would listen to see my love is true.
I long to share the genuineness I feel,
And give to you my love that is so real.

I yearn for you and I always will,
If only you could know the loss I feel.
I know you are the love of my life,
Surely we should let our hearts unite.

I still love you and certainly you loved me,
If only we would let our love be released.
Our long lost love should be open and free,
Forever together just you and me.

She Is Needy

She is searching for love,
She has known only rejection.
She longs to be accepted,
She needs some affection.
She is not cheap, she is needy.

Her morals are not the best,
She appears to be promiscuous.
She does not want the sex,
She is searching for love and happiness.
She is not cheap, she is needy.

She is sometimes called a tramp,
She tries too hard to please.
Though she needs a big hug,
She will settle for a little squeeze.
She is not cheap, she is needy.

Her judgment calls are bad,
She is too quick to say, yes.
She is easily influenced,
She has been terribly abused.
She is not cheap, she is needy.

Her decisions are not rational,
Her needs are emotional.
She lacks self-respect,
She is most vulnerable.
She is not cheap, she is needy.

She needs to love herself,
She believes she is not valuable.
She is short on self-worth,
Consisting of constant work.
She is not cheap, she is needy.

She needed love from the womb,
Nurturing was needed very soon.
She has suffered deprivation,
Now she exhibits compensation.
She is not cheap, she is needy!

Easy On My Eyes

His profession may place him on call,
That will not bother me at all.
I can accept his career compromise,
But let him be easy on my eyes.

He may travel racking up frequent miles,
I can adjust to this different lifestyle.
Though his business is with a franchise,
Please let him be easy on my eyes.

It is significant for me to realize,
I must have a man who is easy on my eyes.
Let him have whatever profession he desires,
But he must be easy on my eyes.

His work hours may be long,
I will support him and be strong.
Though he has his own enterprise,
Please let him be easy on my eyes.

He may give seminars in lecture halls,
Teaching profoundly topics that enthrall.
Though he is accomplished and quite dignified,
Yet let him be easy on my eyes.

He may travel to visit site locations,
I can join him on some occasions.
Though he is an architect who designs,
Still, let him be easy on my eyes.

It is significant that I do realize,
I must have a man who is easy on my eyes.
Let him have whatever profession he desires,
But he must be easy on my eyes.

The Final Decree

The criticisms, the crying,
The accusations, the agonizing,
The discontentment is ruinous,
The tension is stressful to me.

The distrust, the deceiving,
The lying, the lamenting,
The contempt is calamitous,
The anxieties are paralyzing me.

The finances, the faking,
The discord, the dissenting,
The withdrawal is disastrous,
If I stay, where will I be?

The adversities, the anguishing,
The sadness, the suffering,
The isolation is unbearable,
What is this doing to me?

The guilt, the grieving,
The sorrow, the struggling,
The desolation is insufferable,
Though some may disagree.

The pain, the proceedings,
The judgment, the final decree!
The mourning is obvious,
Still, I must set myself free!

This is tearing me apart,
I'm performing surgery on my own heart!
Yet, I must do what is best for me,
I must set myself free!

Valentine's Day

Valentine's Day is a special occasion,
To express ones love and heartfelt devotion.
Lovers share gifts in an affectionate manner,
And bask in romance on this day of enchantment.

Expressions of love are in the atmosphere,
Amorous events are occurring everywhere;
Presenting boxes of chocolates and gorgeous roses,
Giving Valentine cards with romantic poetry.

Winsome couples sharing candlelight dinners,
Bestowing beautiful gifts of loving sentiments;
With serenading music and romantic ballads,
Snuggling closely as they dance slowly together.

Romantic ambiance and adoring lovers,
Enamored with endearing shared affection;
Basking in the glow of warmhearted pleasure,
Knowing these adorable moments will be treasured.

Intimate strolls in beautiful flower gardens,
Smitten with admiration and tender passion;
Placing a gardenia in her lovely hair,
He softly whispers to her, "We're a perfect pair."

Sweethearts endowed with ardent infatuation,
Captivated in their magnetic alluring attraction;
Fascinated by their warm doting seduction,
As they happily lose their hearts to each other.

Valentine's Day romanticizes fanciful excursions,
Beloved sentiments for lovers and dreamers;
Endearment and fondness shared with adoration,
Tender feelings of love shown on this occasion.

Searching For My Significant Other

I'm searching intensely for my significant other,
Evidently, I will have to look quite a bit further.
He has to be accomplished with integrity,
And handsome enough to excite me profoundly.

I know today things have radically changed,
The availability of men is not the same.
Some are taken; others in unique relations,
Yet I'm optimistic there's one to be my companion.

My preferred qualifications are not that unique,
Just handsome and accomplished with integrity.
Why should he be so difficult to find,
I'm certain there are many who are qualified.

Perhaps one day when I least expect it,
He will introduce himself quite casually.
I will be in awe without revealing my surprise,
Thrilled to at last be looking into his eyes.

I will appear serene in the presence of this find,
Confidently, I will be myself at all times.
Conversing interestingly and very refined,
Enjoying a good laugh at appropriate times.

He will tell me important components of his life,
I will genuinely relish the happiness we have derived.
Listening intensely to him as we sit close,
I will share situations that I enjoy the most.

I know he must be around somewhere,
If I knew where to find him, I would be there.
I will search for him from coast to coast,
And believe someday there will be our wedding toast.

Alone, But Not Lonely

Delighting in celestial days,
Basking in serene weekends.
Enjoying blissful ocean side walks,
Planning picnics in scenic parks.

Sailing along in Hawaii,
Catching a show on Broadway.
Relaxing by my swimming pool,
Sending invitations for my barbeque.

Accepting cordial engagements,
Dining at gourmet establishments.
Completing nuptial decorations,
Buying gifts for wedding receptions.

Shopping for a new Jaguar,
Calling friends on the cellular.
Working out all the details,
Planning continental vacations.

Listening to the horses' hooves,
Riding on trails along meadow brooks.
Visiting museums in the early afternoon,
Settling in with my favorite books.

Dashing to shopping malls,
Buying yuletide presents.
Preparing holiday celebrations,
Sharing with friends and relations.

Experiencing all of this flexibility,
Enjoying all of this versatility,
Living a life of creativity,
Alone, but not lonely!

Serial Marriages

I married my first husband because he was the one,
Before I knew it, the marriage had become undone.
My second husband was jolly and so much fun,
Before long, he was the one I wanted to shun.

My third husband was made especially for me,
Before I could count to three, I wanted to be free.
My fourth husband was reserved and very refined,
Before long, I knew he was not the marrying kind.

My fifth husband was my wonderful great find,
Before I knew it, he was awash in liquor and wine.
My sixth husband was gentle and very kind,
Before long, he had a wondering debilitated mind.

My seventh husband was the man of my dreams,
Before I knew it, he was abusive and very mean.
My eighth husband was like a lovable teddy bear,
Before long, he was like a virtual living nightmare.

My ninth husband was just the man I needed,
Before I knew it, I'd rather sleep than see him.
My tenth husband seemed to be my charming prince,
Before long, he was giving me an emotional fit.

My eleventh husband fit me like a sleeve,
Before I knew it, I was frantic for him to leave.
My twelfth husband I knew was just right,
Before long, I didn't want him in my sight.

Quite possibly serial marriages might not be my style,
Perhaps I should give myself a wee bit more time.
On second thought, a husband shouldn't be on my mind,
Perhaps I am best suited just to stay alone for awhile!

Crime In America

The murders,
The maimings,
The carjackings,
The tragedies!
The perpetrators grow younger,
The crimes grow bolder!

What has happened,
To the children?
Have the parents,
Abandoned discipline?
The offenders are more vicious,
The crimes are more malicious!

The child abuse,
The elderly misuse,
The battered wives,
The damaged lives!
The criminals are abstruse,
The crimes are profuse!

The pedophilias,
The pornography,
The child prostitution,
The illegal drug distribution!
The victim manipulation,
The crimes are a preoccupation!

The savings and loan scams,
The military procurement shams,
The high technology criminals,
The business embezzlers!
The congressional schemes,
The white collar crimes are accelerating!

The citizens are prisoners,
With windows and doors barred,
Installing cameras and fences,
Ventures from homes are limited!
The criminal element causes tensions,
What should we anticipate during this century!

Only Thirteen

This was a time when rape was very obscure,
No one heard, though the charge was accurate and true.
She was only thirteen and you were a legal man,
Regretfully, she thought you were a decent family friend.

She asked you for a ride home; you delayed until dark,
You drove her to an isolated dark secluded park.
She fought you furiously with all her youthful strength,
Her lungs were on fire and her heart burned within her chest.

She struggled so hard your car windows were fogged,
You fought her incessantly hard strenuously and long.
Your strength over powered her because she was only a child,
You raped and impregnated her and changed her very life!

Due to her family, she had no voice to say what happened,
She was frozen with fear while terror tore within her.
She did not even know how to label this catastrophe,
Painfully, from that time forward her life was a tragedy.

She was labeled by everyone as being a wayward girl,
This caused her to be ostracized and shunned within her world.
Neighbors asked her, "Why did you do this to your mother?"
She was a victim of a crime that should have put you in Folsom!

She had an exceedingly handsome and wonderful son,
And she suffered for years due to the blight you had done.
Life was very difficult, but it made her very strong,
She obtained university degrees and a profession second to none.

You may have long discarded this crime as nothing,
Yet, she remembers vividly and knows you will be punished.
For God observed everything and it is recorded,
You will stand before Him one day and receive your judgment!

Loving Life

Living very comfortably at long last,
Knowing my future will be brighter than my past.
Enjoying the pleasures I receive each day,
Continuously grateful for God's grace.

Living the wonderful life that I love,
Showered with blessings from above.
Ever relying on God's Word as my light,
Striving daily to walk upright.

Living contented in a tranquil state,
Ecstatic to be out of the employment race.
Wonderfully growing in spiritual ways,
Studying God's Word regularly day-by-day.

Living life happily at my own pace,
Thankful not to have to rush and make haste.
Freedom to do usually whatever I decide,
Having sanctification as my constant guide.

Living quite relaxed without emotional stress,
Most appreciative to have genuine inner-rest.
Cognizant I must live within my means,
Conservative purchases place my mind at ease.

Living a healthy fulfilling lifestyle,
Socializing enjoyably as occasions arise.
Tastefully hosting family and friends,
Sometimes wishing these visits would extend.

Living a serene and flexible life,
Enabling creativity to flow at anytime.
Writing poems that come as a short story,
Experiencing the anointing of God's glory.

Life Everlasting

Salvation was given,
That we may not miss heaven,
Through God's only Son;
By confessing with the mouth,
And believing with the heart.

God so loved the world, you see,
That He gave His only Son for you and me.
And whoever believes in Him, indeed,
Will not perish, but is free,
To have life everlasting!

Where will we reside, one questions,
In the house with many mansions;
For we have proceeded unto life,
Through salvation and sanctification.
This is life everlasting!

The city is pure gold,
Like unto clear glass.
Its walls are adorned,
With precious stones.
Its gates are made of pearls.

Opened will be the books,
With records of all our works.
One will be the Book of Life,
Which names all recipients,
Of a new heaven and a new earth.

God will wipe away every tear,
Death will no more appear;
Nor sorrow, nor crying, it is plain,
There will be no more pain.
There could be no greater gain!

These words are faithful and true,
For He who sits on the throne said,
"Behold, I make all things new."
"I will give of the fountain of the water of life,
Freely to him who thirsts;" this He will do!

Lyrics of Life

Lyrics of Life is a work of art in poems, pictures, and presentation.

The perception and insight of the author are exemplified as you glean through the works in *Lyrics of Life*.

Billie Ambers
Author

The author is a Former Los Angeles Community College District Counselor with a Bachelor of Arts Degree and a Master of Arts Degree in Psychology, from the University of Southern California and Pepperdine University, respectively. She also attended California Lutheran University with a Counseling and Guidance Major in the Master of Science Degree Program.

LYRICS of LIFE PUBLICATIONS
Los Angeles, California 90008

Telephone (323) 792-4446   Facsimile (323) 792-4446

Books Online: www.Amazon.com
E-Mail Address: LyricsOfLife@SBCglobal.net

Majority of pictures by Ed Simpson Photography.

Trademark

Lyrics of Life Publications

ISBN 0-9653400-0-7